Sterling Wit and Wisdom

1,065 Greatest Things Ever Said

by
Steve Sterling
Primus Inter Pares

Sterling Wit and Wisdom
1,065 Greatest Things Ever Said
by Steve Sterling

Copyright © 2024 by Steve Sterling

Published and distributed globally by SLC Publishing.

All right reserved without prejudice worldwide. No part of this book may be reproduced by any mechanical, photographic, or electronic process, or in the form of a phonographic recording; nor may it be stored in a retrieval system (with the exception of a personal eTablet/Reader or personal computer), transmitted, or otherwise be copied for public or private use —other than for "fair use" as brief quotations embodied in articles and reviews without prior express written permission from the publisher. The aphorisms and statements herein may not be made into memes or other forms of publications without the express written permission of the author, and the inclusion of the full name of the author giving credit to his writings.

This book is published under the protection of the First Amendment Freedom of Speech and of the Press pursuant to the Constitution for the United States of America.

ISBN: 978-1-7365590-2-4 eBook. ISBN: 978-1-7365590-3-1 paperback.

First publishing: May 23, 2024

This book was conjured, written, edited, and cover designed by Steve Sterling.

The paperback version of this book may or may not be printed in an automated digital sweatshop by exploited machines that have no rights under local customs, state statutes, federal laws, international treaties, or intergalactic pacts. And that's okay.

Disclaimer: This book was created strictly for entertainment, social commentary, educational, and enlightenment purposes. If you're easily offended by the contents herein, then good! You deserve to be affronted.

Categories:
- Humor & Entertainment › Humor › Puns & Wordplay
- Humor & Entertainment › Humor › Satire
- Nonfiction › Politics & Social Sciences › Philosophy › Modern

Keywords: Humor, Comedy, Wit, Inspirational, Puns, Satire, Quotations, Cynic, Jokes, Parodies, Philosophy, Social Commentary, Modern Madness, Entertainment, Naughty, Sex

Table of Contents

Introduction 5
Wit & Non Sequiturs 8
Money 40
Philosophy 46
Relationships 116
Comedy 123
Random Questions People Have Asked Me 146
    A Little More About Me 160
Increase Your Intelligence 162
Review 163
About The Author 164

Introduction

Being the world's most brilliant, unique, hilarious, daring, and ferociously candid philosopher, wit and pundit of the twenty-first century is not an easy feat to accomplish and sustain (for the competition is formidably fierce indeed), but nonetheless I've managed to adroitly achieve this coveted status with flair, verve, and panache, thanks to my astonishingly intense, mysterious mind with deeply penetrating insights, combined with massive gonads comprised of an undetermined alloy.

As a member of Generation X, I have a unique perspective of life on Earth which is vastly different in many fundamental ways from that of the average person. I started writing aphoristic sayings, philosophical comments, jokes, and other glib, amusing quips in the late 1980s when I was barely old enough to drive and drink, not necessarily in that order. I've been jotting down marvelous epigrams, dazzling ideas, clever word-play, cynical comments, acerbic witticisms, and deeply profound reflections on life for more than three and a half decades.

I could be considered a brash comedian, an outspoken social commentator, occasionally an incorrigible eccentric, frequently an outlandish, obnoxious dissident, a raging rebel, a sarcastic sage, a grumpy geezer, an ineffable anomaly, and even a menace to the very fabricated of society—and sometimes, a crude, rude, lewd, nude dude.

My philosophical observations, sharp insights, introspections, proclamations, and sagacious advice are magnificent and supremely inspirational; they uplift, empower and enlighten others, certainly on par with and mostly surpassing anything else ever written. There are numerous gems of truth embedded in my quotes. My words of wisdom herein are extraordinarily ingenious, wickedly wisely witty, fiercely spot on, exceedingly irreverent, and often shockingly, brutally honest.

Don't ask me why, but I innately revel in desecrating stupid belief systems, lampooning superficiality, mocking morons, satirizing the follies and worst aspects of society, demolishing idiotic behaviors, and gleefully slaughtering sacred cows and profane swine—figuratively speaking, of course. Some of my pithy comments tend to pith off some people. I pull no punches, and punch no pulls, except on Thursdays at half-past three.

The sizzling hot contents of this astounding *rara avis* book range from cleverly playful and funny to strangely surreal, bizarrely absurd and utterly ridiculous to refreshingly sincere and delightfully sublime to outright brutally cynical and darkly impious utterances. Welcome to my scathing satirical realm of harsh, scornful philosophy mixed with amusing clever quips, profound opinions, hysterical comedic comments, and deeply penetrating insights—influenced by such luminaries as Ambrose Bierce, H. L. Mencken, Oscar Wilde, Ashleigh Brilliant, George Carlin, Friedrich Nietzsche, Monty Python, Bill Burr, Jimmy Carr, Rodney Dangerfield, Marcus Aurelius, Roger Bacon, Thomas Paine, Thomas Hobbes, John Locke, Dorothy Parker, Mark Twain, Lao Tzu, Robert Anton Wilson, John Lennon, and Benny Hill.

Some of my witticisms are time-delayed jokes and extraordinarily clever word-play, full of innuendos and out-you-endos, double entendres and occasionally triple entendres. If you don't understand them right away, you'll comprehend them when you start using your frontal lobe for something besides being a passive receptacle of the shallow, asinine, and often insane culture that permeates our late-modern, toxic, chaotic, apocalyptic world.

This potent book is now available without a prescription. Side effects may include chuckles, bursts of laughter, shaking of head and groaning, more laughter, raised eyebrows, gasps, yet more hearty laughter several times, sudden gestalt thinking, possible, probable shock, upset emotions, jealousy, convulsions of anger, and shouts of profanities whilst leaping up and kicking things followed by protracted consternation. One never knows.

I promise that this inimitable book will tickle your cerebral palette like it has never been tickled before (despite this strangely mixed metaphor). That is, if you have a functioning, open mind—preferably with above-average intelligence and a keen sense of humor; that always helps! Within these prized pages of this high-value, rare and marvelous manuscript are one thousand and sixty-five of my mirthful comments, amazing aphorisms, awesomely clever observations, and epic fannies...uh, I mean, epiphanies, yeah, epiphanies—that's the word.

Additionally, there are not one, not two, but three free bonus sections of my personal gift wish list, random questions people have asked me and my startling, hilarious, and sometimes shocking answers, and finally a quick technique to immediately increase your intelligence.

So, sit back and devour this exceptionally unique work of my original quotes that I created, contrived, conjured and crafted over decades. But be forewarned! Once you read this stupendous, dynamic book, the contents will be in your mind forever, and you will never be the same again. Ever.

And, finally, don't take it all too seriously. Keep in mind, they're only letters of the alphabet arranged my way.

Magnanimously,

Steve Sterling

Wit & Non Sequiturs

1
During a brainstorm, I got struck with enlightening.

2
It is better to be a catalyst than a dogmatist.

3
My computer crashed. I shouldn't be driving it on the street anyway.

4
Kiss My Arsenal!

5
Party hard! It's better than partying limp.

6
If you join more than one sect, you will have sects day and night.

7
A bird in the hand is worth getting into her bush.

8
I believe in going the extra mile as long as I'm chauffeured in a limousine with a wet bar.

8

9
I've never met my equal, but if I ever do, I'll congratulate the lucky bastard.

10
Why does the word 'funeral' begin with the word 'fun'?

11
I'm a morning person, after 9 AM.

12
The smarter you become, the more you realize just how insanely stupid so many people are.

13
Although I easily qualify for membership, I have no interest in joining Mensa; too many members have immensa egos.

14
I have a sensor from a censor to censure the senseless in a sensible way.

15
Once I'm cremated, I'll make an ash out of myself.

16
I must admit that I am occasionally shockingly vulgar, but in a sophisticated, diplomatic, and even charming way.

17
I'm a time traveler, one minute at a time.

18
Don't judge a conspiracy book by its cover-up.

19
Birds of a feather shag each other.

20
Why is smoke holy?

21
On the road to ruin, substance abuse is the scenic route.

22
Power to the People! (But only to those with working brains and pleasant personalities.)

23
I'm not greedy; I'm merely rapaciously accelerating my assets acquisitions.

24
A word is worth one-thousandth of a picture.

25
I can be a writer, at least write now, because I know my writes, and I'm write on the money.

26
Sixty is the new fifty-nine, and ninety is the new seventy.

27
Murphy's Law is true, and Murphy was a keen optimist.

28
Where do seed sellers get the seeds of seedless fruits and vegetables?

29
I'm highly allergic to manual labor.

30
In quantum physics, the past is now, and the future isn't what it used to be.

31
The hummingbird is my favorite bird. My other favorite birds wear short skirts and high heels.

32
I may not be perfect, but my flaws are amazingly superior and downright impressive.

33
82.7% of all statistics are false and made-up on the spot, including this one.

34
At some point in life, almost every person has asked the big question: "Why are we here?" The answer is: because we're not over there.

35
No man is an island, but I've done rather well as a jutting peninsula.

36
Chocolate is like legal cocaine for women.

37
As you sew, so shall you rip.

38
A musical instrument can be a sound investment.

39
Liposuction is a surgical technique that sucks the American out of a person.

40
I didn't sleep my way to the top; I was awake the whole time.

41
When I was in school, the part of campus where I invested the most time was the hippocampus.

42
Some rock stars are guilty of playing airhead guitar.

43
If you lose your erection, don't be so hard on yourself.

44
Be aloof. The world needs more loofs.

45
I'm ambidextrous: I write with my right hand, and I left with my left hand.

46
Since I've given up all superstitious delusions, I feel much better.

47
You can take your narcissistic gaslighting and shove it up your gas hole.

48
Not to brag, but I was faithful to my spouse on numerous occasions.

49
The world is your toxins-tainted oyster.

50
I'll find the secret of immortality even if it kills me!

51
Do the so-called 'wages of sin' adjust to accommodate inflation and deflation?

52
Why be deadpan when you can be dead skillet?

53
With friends like that, who needs enemas?

54
Speak softly and wield a big willy.

55
I live in the future, which is why I'm always arriving in the now.

56
I have a really long Do List and even lengthier Don't List.

57
Smokers make ashes of themselves.

58
A leftist and its capital are soon parted.

59
You're not narrow-minded, and nothing I say or do will convince you otherwise.

60
Can a leopard change its spots? Yes, with new and improved spot remover.

61
My concupiscence runneth over.

62
I was driven to drink; then I got smart and had it driven to me instead.

63
If you must lie, at least be honest about it.

64
The Pleiades Constellation is 541 Light Years away, give or take a kilometer.

65
As you smoke, so shall you reek.

66
Flattery is the sincerest form of irritation.

67
When taking a crash course in driving lessons, be a wreck-less driver, not a reckless driver.

68
The pen is mightier than the sword, except when one is fencing.

69
Does root beer float?

70
Don't look a gift horse in the mouth, or in any other orifice.

71
I really dig archaeology.

72
As an archaeologist, I used to date ancient artefacts. Then I started dating young ladies instead.

73
I still practice safe sex. I'm hoping to one day get it right.

74
When I was accused of putting on a front, I was taken aback.

75
I don't wear a tinfoil hat. My hat is 24 karat gold adorned with jewels, platinum antennae, built-in radio transmitter, and music player with a one-million-song playlist.

76
"Do you know the muffin man?" Not intimately.

77
I broke the four-minute mile into several pieces.

78
At college, I joined the IV League. In addition to drinking, we received alcohol through an IV.

79
Conjugate the verve.

80
May all your screams come true.

81
I remember that I failed to recall what is was that I wasn't supposed to forget, but I know nothing of whatever it wasn't that I didn't do.

82
My laurel is hardy.

83
Armed with the sword of wisdom, the shield of truth, the helmet of inspiration, and the codpiece of audacity, we shall prevail.

84
I'm not lazy; I'm simultaneously exceedingly unmotivated and energy conserving.

85
Ask not what your country can do for you, but what all of you can do for me.

86
Nobody's perfect, and I'm doing my best to set an example.

87
After etymologists argue, they usually remain on good terms.

88
"Pardon me!" said the sneezing criminal to the judge.

89
I want to be a teleporting kleptomaniac.

90
I'm drug-free, which means I get all my drugs for free.

91
He's so full of shit that it would take weeks to beat it all out of him.

92
I'm a people person, as long as I don't have to interact with them.

93
I may not believe in astrology, but it believes in me.

94
Greed is the fodder of economics. I have no idea who the mudder is.

95
I got fed up with working for myself, so I quit before I could get fired.

96
If an eye for an eye makes the whole world blind, will a tooth for a tooth make the entire world need dentures?

97
I'd rather be an increment than an excrement.

98
The Los Angeles Breatharian Society: air today, gone tomorrow.

99
I have a PHD: Positively Huge Dinger.

100
I think parenthetically (but not always).

101
I don't want to complain, but why break a beloved family tradition?

102
I love beautiful women's butts so much that I'm an ass-ficianado.

103
People need more standup comity.

104
So much education, so little wisdom.

105
528 Hertz so good.

106
Freethinker–with every purchase!

107
I have a list of every list I have.

108
Would someone please call me an amulet?

109
Some of my best friends are non sequiturs.

110
The Big Apple is rotten to the core and not a-peeling.

111
I broke the sabbath, in thirteen places.

112
With so much to achieve, who has time for mere work?

113
If you can eat haggis, you can 'stomach' anything.

114
I like horticulture, but I prefer a cultured whore.

115
I have so much personal magnetism that, every December 25th, I give charisma presence.

116
I eat, therefore I yam.

117
I talk to myself because I'm such a fabulous conversationalist and entirely agreeable with myself.

118
I'd rather be naughty than naught.

119
It's better to be chuffed than to be cuffed (unless you're into kinky acts).

120
Some Muslims are full of Shiite.

121
It's better than a poke in the stick with a sharp eye.

122
I was chaste all over town.

123
Why is it called a 'Spelling Bee'? Bee Cause, that's why.

124
Not to be rhetorical, but what does bimbo want?

125
Sex, sex, sex is the number of the best.

126
It takes gall to be a Gaul.

127
The first time I astral projected, I was completely beside myself.

128
Change is afoot, sometimes a hand, and occasionally ahead.

129
I've spent so much money buying classical music recordings, that I'm flat baroque.

130
When I got her pregnant, it was like taking baby from a candy.

131
I have a peaceful, humble, acquiescent, live-and-let-live attitude, and I'll brutally slaughter anybody who doesn't agree with this.

132
I went from Teen-hope to Twenty-nothing to Thirty-something to Forty-most-anything to Fifty-Fuck-All!

133
I support our dupes.

134
Be genuine, even if you aren't.

135
He let whatever good looks he had go to his head with a brain that he didn't have.

136
We mustn't let sleeping dogs lie; we should wake them up and force them to be truthful.

137
Ply me with enough drugs and/or alcohol, and I can handle almost any crisis.

138
I've got to take a massive Shit List.

139
A funeral is a grave event.

140
I'm a New Wage Guru.

141
Your dogma pooped on my spiritual path, so my karma ran over your dogma.

142
From Manifest Destiny to Man Infest Density.

143
The best success is revenge, or something like that!

144
Last of the Indigenous.

145
With Islamic extremists, it's Allah nothing.

146
Got a way with words, and got away with murder.

147
Gotu Kola, and don't come back.

148
You're cordially invited to join the 1%…Nah, just kidding. They despise you.

149
Analyze anal lies.

150
Some of what I said in Japan was Rost In Tlansration.

151
Her visage is so hideous, it could stop a train.

152
Communism is full of Bolshevik.

153
The first time I laid eyes on her, I wanted to lay more than my eyes on her.

154
I live such an extremely awesome natural lifestyle, that I'm super natural.

155
It's better to be poly-amorous than Pollyanna.

156
I must admit, I am a wit. At least I'm not a stupid git.

157
Lately neither the spirit nor the flesh is eager.

158
With wisdom, comes age, or something like that.

159
Love is in the air. So is the stench of flatulence.

160
May the person I hate be reincarnated as a late-term abortion, and then a disease-ridden pinworm in a swine's stool sample.

161
Many people want to have out-of-body experiences. If they would patiently wait until they're dead, they'll have all the out-of-body experience that they can handle.

162
To use a Spoonerism, you're a Shining Wit.

163
Seek Rhett in telly, Gents.

164
Every man and every woman is a czar, and I'm being czarcastic.

165
He's not paranoid! They really *are* after him!

166
When it comes to fondling beautiful young ladies, I have plenty of hands-on experience.

167
The guitarist said to the keyboardist, "I don't have pianist envy."

168
She went from an hourglass figure to over four hours.

169
I joke for pun and profit.

170
Succeed or suck egg—the choice is yours.

171
When I die, instead of a somber, boring funeral, I want people to hold a traditional Irish Wake, because being thrown a wake is better than being thrown asleep.

172
European. I'm a-peein'. We're all a-peein'.

173
A geologist's favorite mixed drink is a Gin and Tectonic.

174
I despise gambling. Years ago, at a casino, I lost a nickel, and I'm still looking for it.

175
Copper wire was invented when two of my Scottish ancestors found the same penny at the same time.

176
I can get a lot done when I don't have so much menial work to do.

177
I found out that I'm part Asian, but I don't know which part.

178
I don't do drugs. They do me.

179
I'm rather congenial, which is better than being congenital.

180
Many people are alcoholics. I'm an aquaholic.

181
I can easily walk on water—when it's frozen.

182
I have a magnetic personality with the opposite polarity, so I repel a lot of people.

183
I should get paid interest for making sperm bank deposits.

184
I was caught vigorously masticating in a public restaurant.

185
Enough of impersonators! There's only one Elvis! Any more than one would be bloody unbearable.

186
I don't steal. I permanently borrow.

187
She made accusations that my horn transposed into the crescendo of her orchestra pit.

188
It's better to have a date with Destiny than with Chastity, because Chastity doesn't put out, but Destiny sure does!

189
Many are called, but most are wrong numbers.

190
You can lie down or you can lie standing up; the choice is yours.

191
Windows are a pane in the glass.

192
If some people have thick accents, do others have thin accents?

193
May your career take off and never come back.

194
Oh, for the good old days when men were men and women were stoic pugilists.

195
A boiled kettle never watches.

196
When it comes to tarot, it's six of wands, half a dozen the other.

197
I met a woman so obese that she gave berth to a ship.

198
The three stages of male mental development are infancy, puerility, and senility.

199
Intelligent people seem crazy to the unwise.

200
I disowned myself.

201
This idea does not exist.

202
I'm so outrageous that I'm inrageous.

203
I live to eat, but only when I'm hungry.

204
I'm proud of my hair. I grew it organically myself and I'm rather attached to it.

205
I don't remember that rock concert like it was yesterday; that's because I wasn't there.

206
I have photogenic memory.

207
CBS = See B.S.

208
I am full of pith.

209
They say laughter is contagious, but so are many diseases.

210
If I had my way, I'd have my way.

211
I'm into casual sex, but I also like invitation-only Black-Tie formal intercourse.

212
Abstinence makes the hard grow fonder, and the fond grow harder.

213
Laugh at yourself; everyone else does.

214
Better laid than never.

215
There's more to me than meets the I.

216
Don't let wanking get out of hand.

217
Homeward bound and gagged.

218
I believe in climax change.

219
Oh, the vexations and perils of writing brilliant, original, unique epigrams for a functionally-illiterate, dumbed-down society.

220
With Bono singing, it's hard to get a word in Edge-wise.

221
I'm not against rap; I prefer music.

222
Dope springs eternal.

223
We aim to police.

224
My enemies and I are polar opposites; for example, I'm highly intelligent, good-looking, suave, witty, virile, and successful.

225
It's not that I'm so much smarter than many people; it's that countless others are so aggravatingly stupid!

226
I may be absolutely mad, but only part-time.

227
I've learnt an awful lot, and a lot of it was awful.

228
He's blind. That's why we don't see eye-to-eye.

229
There's a cure for Mad Cow Disease: a dozen roses and a box of chocolates.

230
One nuclear bomb explosion can ruin your whole day.

231
They're called 'character actors', as opposed to other actors with no character.

232
Why do you call your tea 'Oolong'? Because it's not Oo-short.

233
When meditating and chanting mantras, there's no place like Om.

234
I'm not racist. I hate everyone equally, and some more than others.

235
Good things come in pears, but they also come in other fruit.

236
My favorite Asian dish is Chiks Tu Yung (but not too young for me).

237
Does a woman who's giving birth labor in vain?

238
I am ruthless because there's no Ruth in my life.

239
Australia started as the world's largest penile colony.

240
I went to a Buddhist Temple to find a single girl who's exquisitely Buddha-full.

241
Give a shit!
No thanks. I gave at the orifice.

242
It's better to be New Age than old age.

243
Kiss my onus.

244
I shall live forever in your hearts, and other body parts.

245
With impunity I defecate upon his heinous visage.

246
I don't close-caption my wit for the intellectually-challenged or humor-debilitated.

247
Since I believe in reincarnation, I won't even step on an ant, because today's ant could be tomorrow's uncle.

248
As an author, I have the write of way.

249
The end is near, and the beginning is now.

250
A clinical study confirms that five out of four people are bad at fractions, and eleven out of ten of them are gullible idiots.

251
It's okay for a Taurus to be full of bull.

252
As a Scorpio, it's my prerogative (and purgative) to be an All-or-Nothing personality.

253
I'm armed to the teeth with teeth in my arms.

254
I have the answer to your solution and the problem to your question.

255
Those who have eyes will hear and those with ears will see.

256
I'm royalty. There's no need to genuflect; just give your tax and tributes to me, and everything will be fine.

257
Why would anyone go to hell in a handbasket when they can take public transportation?

258
Ships are referred to as 'she' and 'her' because they're vessels to be filled with worthy seamen.

259
There's nothing new under the Sun, except the latest software version update.

260
There wouldn't be food shortages if we ate our vegetables, fruits and nuts instead of electing them.

261
God save the Queen, or what's left of her.

262
Is 'Microsoft' a description of its founder's penis?

263
When it comes to texting, I'm all thumbs.

264
Remember, no one can predict the future except psychics who never win the lottery.

265
My preferred pronouns are "Lord God", also "Your Majesty".

266
I had a paradox, and am now down to just one dox.

267
I want to catch a fly using chopsticks, but I've never seen a fly actually use chopsticks.

Money

268
The love of money is the root of all normalcy.

269
If money is the root of all evil, why do churches continuously ask for more of it?

270
I love money far more than I like most humans, because I never met a dollar that was a stupid asshole.

271
When you are an employee, you are someone's bitch making them rich.

272
Money is a human-made fabrication which you must work for when you have scant of it, and which will work for you when you wield a hefty sum of it.

273
Nothing gives satisfaction the way being rich does.

274
Money is silent, but it speaks volumes.

275
Master your finances, or they will master you.

276
'Tis better to be a rich snob than a poor slob.

277
I gave up poverty; there's no money in it.

278
Credit cards: buy now, pay and pain later.

279
"Money doesn't buy happiness" is the rich person's snide, condescending consolation for the poor. Money and plenty of it does buy happiness, if you know where to shop and who to rent.

280
Even some of the rich are consumed by the system that they support.

281
The Japanese have quite a yen for money, and so do I.

282
Confucius might have said, "Man who doesn't tend business tends to lose business."

283
For the entrepreneur, life is tedious and dreary when working for someone else.

284
There's no such thing as excessive wealth, only excessive unrealized ambition.

285
When you're wealthy, no one cares what your high school or college GPA was.

286
Charity begins at home, which is why I give generously to myself.

287
The deal is not finished until the check clears the bank.

288
Life's too short for poverty.

289
Feed your need and greed.

290
If you want to become rich, do not toil to gain riches; rather, engage others to toil for you. Leverage your time.

291
Some poor people appreciate possessions that depreciate in value.

292
The greatest secret to wealth and power is this: do you know how stupid most people are? Well, the average person is even dumber than that.

293
Never do tasks on your own time which you can do on someone else's time, and get paid for it.

294
Consuming alcohol over many years can cost over half a million dollars. Do you know what the price of a liver transplant surgery is these days?

295
If the love of money really is the root of all evil, then I have an enormous, unquenchable taproot.

296
There is no such thing as disposable income. If you want to dispose of your income, give it all to me.

297
Money may or may not buy happiness, but it is a passport to pleasures.

298
The quantity of tattoos on a person is usually inversely proportionate to their financial intelligence.

299
Do you want to get rich? Billions of daft, gullible people want to give their money to others. If you want to be successful in business, you only need convince enough fools to give their money to you, then you will be rich.

300
You're making more money than you've ever made before–and that's not saying much.

301
I've grown my hair really long for locks of love: I love saving money so much that I don't get my locks cut.

302
It's a husband's job to make money, and a wife's responsibility to relieve him of it.

303
Jesus saves, but does he earn interest?

304
It's my moral obligation to relieve fools of their money.

305
I invest in stocks and bondage.

306
Keep building yourself and your business until you have a retinue of obsequious sycophants who have helped you become wealthy.

307
A high net worth gives a happy heart.

Philosophy

308
Enjoy being in joy.

309
With the abundance of bullshit in this crazy world, we can build a Stairway to Heaven.

310
The wrong book can waste your time and achieve nothing. The right book can change your life and the course of history.

311
The path to greatness is never easy, but it is well worth the efforts.

312
Follow no one. Lead yourself.

313
Instead of divide and conquer, it's time to be divine and concur.

314
I have a simple philosophy: if it's not bringing me wealth, health, happiness, inspiration, or screaming orgasms, it doesn't belong in my life.

315
The people who don't appreciate you should not be allowed to be with you.

316
You cannot alter the past, but you can create your future by living in the present moment; that's where your power is.

317
Surround yourself with luxury, not negativity.

318
You can learn much when you are willing to be still, with your mind quiet and attentive to your intuition.

319
You are here, but not for long.

320
The truth will set you free, but it might upset you for free.

321
The wise lead the way to truth, while the fools follow the herd to slaughter.

322
Whenever I hear someone say they're 'killing time' or they have a certain amount of time 'to kill', I cringe. Your time is your most precious, irreplaceable asset. Anyone who 'kills time' doesn't value their own life.

323
Why wait for opportunity when you can create it?

324
Common sense is now uncommon.

325
Great achievements break the model of impossibility.

326
Language communicates with your mind. Music speaks to your soul.

327
Putting myself first is the best decision I ever made.

328
Ignoring the truth does not negate it.

329
Memories are the only things we have left of the moments. Take advantage of each moment. You'll never get them again.

330
It is better to relieve stress than to relive it.

331
If you've been loyal to the wrong people, make a change. Be loyal to yourself.

332
People show their true personalities with their Halloween costumes.

333
Some people are content creators, others are discontent instigators.

334
If you cannot establish dominance, you can at least create ambiance.

335
When your soul is sick, no drugs will heal it.

336
Instead of fighting disease, focus on healing.

337
Instead of fighting poverty, focus on prosperity.

338
Too often a harshly critical intellect cannot perceive simple truths.

339
If you're not happy with your life, change the program of your bio-computer.

340
Evolve now and avoid the rush.

341
Life is like the lottery: you have to pay and play to win.

342
Get tough or get stuffed.

343
Gold is my favorite heavy metal.

344
Be courageous, not a conformist.

345
Respect worthwhile traditions, but do not be rigidly bound by them.

346
The meaning of life is important; so is a life of meaning.

347
You are not here to be taught that you are separate. You are here to realize that you are connected and a part of the whole.

348
You can tell a lot about a person by the books they don't read.

349
I'm not arrogant, I'm supremely confident.

350
I practice turning the other cheek—of my foe.

351
I like competition. It gives me something to destroy.

352
People like me are not highly offensive. We bluntly tell the truth and many people cannot handle that.

353
I'm all for a monarchy as long as *I'm* the monarch!

354
Your true intelligence is not assessed by an I.Q. test, but by your decisions and actions.

355
Those who show no interest in self-development are those who need it most.

356
Those who would reform others should reform themselves.

357
I'm not highly educated. I'm highly intelligent. There is a difference.

358
It's not Ultimate Fighting unless it's multiple opponents to the death.

359
No matter what you say or do, there's always going to be one or more negative people denigrating you, so do what you want and flaunt it.

360
We should cast aside our differences, and embrace our commonalities.

361
How to effectively deal with toxic, manipulative, abusive, evil narcissists? Daily floggings and biannual crucifixions are historically-proven to be highly effective.

362
Power and profits seem to frequently dissipate environmental responsibility.

363
Today's excelling students are often the ones who've deduced what answers the educators wish to receive.

364
Food affects your mood.

365
Attempting to obtain welfare is often a full-time job.

366
When you let go of your density, you can fulfill your destiny.

367
Your life is like a movie. If it's bad, fire the cast, rewrite the script, and be your own director.

368
There are those who have faith in a government that has no faith in them.

369
Preconceptions are, more often than not, misconceptions.

370
Almost all old people in the U.S. are pillheads.

371
Most people don't critically, independently think; they merely reshuffle and regurgitate their ignorant beliefs, biases, and worthless opinions that they never re-examined.

372
Knowing thyself can be a shocking experience.

373
Having a near-death experience is better than being in a near-life existence.

374
Many humans have entered the twenty-first century with a Dark Ages mentality.

375
The quality of art and music exemplifies the standards of the society from which they are born.

376
There are people who must be defeated in order to win them over.

377
This generation considers extreme abnormality to be normal.

378
If a person needs alcohol in order to have fun, they have a severe personality deficit.

379
All the world may be a stage, but many people are acting terribly, some are not acting at all, and more than a few have miserably failed the audition.

380
Inner child therapy should concentrate on spanking inner brats.

381
I don't have to actively seek unacculturated humans. They're ubiquitous.

382
Why are so many people so tired when they've been asleep all their lives?

383
Consciousness is so absolutely fascinating, yet so few people seem even remotely interested in it; perhaps they haven't fully experienced it.

384
After thousands of years, mankind is still squabbling and warring over real estate.

385
Humanity was a good idea; too bad it failed.

386
What some people won't do to exploit one another and destroy Nature.

387
With the right cannabis strain, there's no such state as being too high.

388
Blessed are the peacemakers, for they shall smoke peace pipes and get high.

389
Some people are updated; others are antiquated.

390
Conform to Individualism!

391
There is no tap-out in real combat.

392
"Trust me" translated accurately means "fuck you!"

393
It only takes one person to start a revolution, but many people to quell it.

394
I found God! He was in the mirror the whole time.

395
Authentic Philosophy is the love of wisdom. Neo Philosophy is the blind devotion to often erroneous Belief Systems that, when abbreviated, are B.S.

396
Anything that is truly beneficial to humanity without generating a profit for a select few is either brutally suppressed, made illegal, or viciously debunked, or all three.

397
Stupidity is a luxury that humanity cannot afford.

398
Some people conceal their intelligence well.

399
Genius is limited, but stupidity seems never-ending.

400
Don't tolerate intolerance.

401
I only have contempt for the contemptuous.

402
The U.S. has become a more classless country—many have no class at all.

403
The pursuit of happiness is a much-invoked but seldom judicially-upheld ideal.

404
Courts have people swear to tell the truth. This is absurd considering that honest people will tell the truth without an oath, and dishonest people will lie regardless.

405
Why are we here? To end as rotting protoplasm?

406
Living is simple, but it isn't easy.

407
If life gives you lemons, eat some, juice some, give some away, keep lots of seeds, and sell the rest of the lemons for a profit.

408
A major accomplishment is a greater pleasure than brief sensual indulgence.

409
Life can be like heavy traffic—more stopping than moving.

410
If life begins at conception, does it end at misconception?

411
Some fashion statements should never have been made.

412
Humans are often clever, but seldom wise. We dream and scheme of conquering each other, the Earth, and outer space, but almost all of us have yet to master our own selves.

413
Language defines, then confines.

414
Today will be yesterday, tomorrow.

415
It's amazing what one can achieve when unhindered by laws, regulations, codes, dogma, morals, and ethics.

416
True peace is not enforced outwardly, but embraced inwardly.

417
Beware of unanswered questions and even more so of unquestioned answers.

418
Avoid those who talk much, yet say little. To convey truth does not require many words.

419
If you must have a one-track mind, do keep it on the right track.

420
Every person is a work of art, because each is an original.

421
If Absolutism is Relative, is Relativism Absolute?

422
Many ill people are so brainwashed that they would staunchly rather have a conformist death than an unconventional cure. I say good riddance to them.

423
Don't let intellect stand in the way of wisdom.

424
Moderation may not be much fun, but it's better in the long run.

425
How does one remain true to a changing self?

426
So many people forego the top floor penthouse, and instead, choose debasement.

427
There is no law against composing and performing music that is utterly devoid of originality and beauty. Therefore, most of today's 'music' is perfectly legal.

428
Some humor should be taken seriously, some stern statements should be ridiculed, and people with no sense of humor should be pranked and laughed at.

429
There are those who believe that they attain absolute enlightenment by realizing that there is no absolute enlightenment.

430
It's impossible to be your own worst enemy when you are your own best friend.

431
Should people serve an ideology, or should an ideology serve people?

432
I am, therefore I think. I thought, therefore I was.

433
If you lose your mind, where does it go?

434
As long as we have warriors, and funders for them, there will be war.

435
Time is malleable according to one's perception of it.

436
Truth is not democratic.

437
For a physically attractive egotist, disengaging one's own charm is a difficult task.

438
Are you insecure about your insecurities?

439
Euthanize Dogma.

440
I don't want cataracts. I want cathartic acts.

441
You were wrong, and I admit it.

442
The idea that nothing is shocking should in itself be shocking.

443
Don't judge a leader by all of their followers.

444
Avoid those of self-perpetuated misery.

445
Often the best conversation is no conversation.

446
I come from a dysfunctional planet.

447
I'm wise enough to confess my ignorance.

448
By what standards do you judge my standards?

449
I'm sure there are numerous things that I don't know. Unfortunately, I know not what they are.

450
I'm outrageously provocative, but all in good fun.

451
I breathe for a living.

452
It is better to be a Master Manifester than a masturbator.

453
It's hard to be positive and successful when one's family are ultra-toxic, narcissistic, insanely dysfunctional, exceedingly stupid assholes.

454
Science could engineer a gene that would eliminate scientists who engineer genes.

455
When it came to assessing humanity, Darwin's only mistake was omitting the letter 'd' from 'evolution'.

456
Say friend, can you spare twelve dollars for a cup of latte with extra stuff on it from $tarbux?

457
I wonder why I wonder.

458
Some people waste their entire lives in pursuit of trivia.

459
Never put off until tomorrow what you can defer for several days or avoid doing altogether.

460
People who attempt to stand out from the crowd often end up creating a new throng of mindless clones.

461
Blessed aren't they who follow silly fads, for they shall go nowhere.

462
The combatant who loses control of him/herself loses control of the fight.

463
I could be wrong, but I'm not.

464
Within Magick, there is Science. Within Science, there is Magick.

465
Just because someone is 'cute' doesn't make them more or less deserving of people's attention.

466
The authors who wrote obscurely have rightly become obscure.

467
The dreams and ideals of youth are often vanquished by the traumas and cynicism of adulthood.

468
Where there's a Will, there's not only a way, but there's also a contentious beneficiary, a legal loophole, and an avaricious lawyer to exploit it.

469
Don't choose indecisiveness.

470
With an increase in audio recording technology has come a parallel decrease in musical creativity and originality.

471
Expand your lexis and you'll expand your knowledge.

472
The totality of human experience is but a mere fraction of the divine.

473
Go from hypnosis to Hip Gnosis.

474
If only the past were as wet clay to be remolded.

475
Dairy farmers pour the milk, while politicians milk the poor.

476
Being late is not fashionable.

477
It's not easy being right almost all the time, but somehow, I manage.

478
A scientist's pride in its objectivity is sometimes in exact proportion to its presumptions and prejudices.

479
Where ends the labyrinth of the mind?

480
Don't judge me too harshly until your consciousness has sufficiently experienced perception of 'reality' through my traumatized receptor organs.

481
Plan on modifying your plans.

482
Whoever said 'silence is golden' obviously wasn't deaf.

483
Temptation can manifest in the subtlest forms.

484
What are the evolutionary functions of ugliness, stupidity, baldness, pubic hair, and nipples on men?

485
We're all savages beneath the cloak of civility.

486
Curtailed creativity can give birth to cynic's mockery.

487
In all things, verify, falsify, or label as indeterminate.

488
Quantifying creativity leads to futility.

489
A form of slavery today is had under the guise of conveniences.

490
You cannot help others if you cannot help yourself.

491
The first trauma in life is birth. After this, things get worse.

492
Knowledge is useless without the resources to apply it.

493
One well-placed verbal barb wounds more than a dozen common profanities.

494
Sometimes amour meets armour.

495
To fully understand and appreciate me, one needn't be a genius, but it certainly helps immensely.

496
One person's morals are another person's inconveniences.

497
Critics vanish; classics endure.

498
How big is God's willy?

499
There are those who think we exist to find out why we exist.

500
Misguided idealism is incompatible with harsh reality.

501
If you have but one true, loyal friend who is still alive when you die, you are extremely lucky.

502
The diligent and the indolent eventually have the same fate: death.

503
The struggle to exist leaves little time to live.

504
Well-meaning ignorance is forgivable. Chronic stupidity is not.

505
I've taken a vow of silence: I vow to silence my enemies.

506
The body can be as much a prison as a temple.

507
It's lonely at the top because most people are content with being at the bottom.

508
Ironic that the military exists for preserving freedom, yet contains little of it.

509
The nuclear family has been disarmed.

510
If the premise that life's journey is more important than the destination, then why have a destination?

511
Most mainstream magazines and newspapers are suitable only for house-training pets and lining the bottoms of bird cages.

512
It is better to be a health nut than an unhealthy nut.

513
I don't give a monkey's backside what Simon Cowbell thinks.

514
I don't mind accommodating others' desires as long as I get my way every time.

515
It is better to be a man of leisure than a man of leisure suits.

516
Humans are born crying. How appropriate.

517
Anyone can assume authority, but few people will accept responsibility and accountability.

518
Most people have not yet discovered the difference between programmed subconscious behavioral patterns, and actions of true conscious free will.

519
Attempting to enlighten people whose ignorance inflames their arrogance is a daunting task that is not worth the hassle. It's much easier to ignore and avoid them.

520
So many premises, so little proof.

521
Transform your trance form.

522
Making the world safe for democracy does not make democracy safe for the world.

523
Some people spend their entire lives planning their entire lives.

524
Beware of locking horns with a closed mind.

525
I'm not asking for much—just for everything to be perfect every moment of every day.

526
For every action, there's a horde of reactionaries.

527
Hers was the face that sunk a thousand ships.

528
Never attack an enemy unless you are prepared to endure and win the war.

529
Real masculinity is non-toxic.

530
A comprehensive martial art seamlessly embraces both internal and external aspects, the absence of either renders combat abilities incomplete.

531
The path of least resistance leads to stasis.

532
Life is relentlessly revised, often by the most vexatious of editors.

533
Junk food. Junk body. Junk mind. Junk life.

534
Extreme evils are hatched by the worst people who believe they are doing the right thing.

535
Grant the original premise, no matter how ludicrous, and every such claim makes sense to the unwise.

536
Billions of dollars are smilingly given to foreign nations and illegal invaders, and only chump change remains for beleaguered, abused citizens.

537
Not every addiction appears in a urinalysis.

538
One person's so-called dangerous weed is another person's proven safe medicinal herb.

539
State-of-the-art sexist: some disassembly required.

540
Imagination and creativity are inspired, not taught.

541
Silence never betrayed anyone.

542
Friends may come, and friends may go, but enemies last a lifetime.

543
The individual is more important than society, for the individual can exist without society, but society cannot exist without individuals.

544
The media tells people what to think and do, and what not to think and not to do.

545
Health is something which people abuse and take for granted until deprived of it.

546
We're all organic: we grow at different rates.

547
Cut, burn, and poison: ancient torture techniques, and conventional cancer treatments.

548
Orthodox thinking produces orthodox results.

549
Human advancement is often severely limited, especially by humans.

550
Give up your wrongs, not your rights!

551
Conformity to stupidity breeds autocracy.

552
Soft rock is like a soft cock: it doesn't satisfy.

553
A selective memory is an act of shrouding and ignoring a multitude of wrongs.

554
If you can't be happy, complain somewhere else.

555
Transform base life through spiritual alchemy.

556
The persistence of excellence is arduous, but the rewards can be great.

557
Without the truth, the brightest mind is vanity.

558
Some people are innately intelligent; others are merely educated.

559
Cream and scum are alike in that both rise to the top.

560
One cannot reason with the irrational.

561
Don't confuse a brain being the same as a mind. A corpse has a brain. A living person, a soul, has a mind.

562
Oppression is the opiate of the Marxists.

563
Why pledge allegiance to a piece of cloth?

564
The Hippocratic Oath has been replaced by the hypocrite lies.

565
Expect nothing and you're never disappointed.

566
You know you're a major musical success when your song is parodied by Weird Al.

567
Those who cling to the past end up with dust and mold as a result.

568
My opinion is neither humble nor arrogant; it just is.

569
Context is crucial.

570
You can lead people to wisdom, but you can't make them think.

571
They lie who vociferously claim they are honest.

572
The best assassins never reveal their secrets.

573
For every problem remedied by science and technology, more problems are created.

574
The easy way out often isn't.

575
Life is like hand-to-hand combat; both are unpredictable.

576
Hope deferred is cruel and usual punishment.

577
A critic's work is never ending.

578
We all need to feel appreciated; some of us prefer it in the form of gifts of large sums of money.

579
Don't blame me for your corrupt politicians; I didn't vote for any of them.

580
It's better to be a legalist than an illegalist.

581
Imprecision in language begets misunderstanding and confusion.

582
Almost anyone can join a gang, but few can start one and effectively manage it.

583
Don't equate bulk with power.

584
Verbosity indicates stupidity.

585
No living language remains static.

586
In concentration camps, there are no obese humans with alleged metabolism problems.

587
Trust no one wearing a tie or a badge.

588
Never let emotions rule your business decisions.

589
I'm not an atheist; I'm an agnostic anti-theist.

590
If it works, it's true. If it's true, doesn't necessarily make it morally right.

591
My idea of Happy Hour is staying home. I'm happy the price is low, it lasts more than an hour, and I never drive drunk.

592
Many of today's carefree, shallow, social media attention whores are tomorrow's washed-up, irrelevant service industry wage slaves.

593
What say we discuss the War On Drugs while we have booze, cigarettes, and prescription pills that kill thousands of people every year?

594
Allopathic doctors practice medicine because they haven't got it right yet.

595
To succeed in Hollywood, it's not who you know, but who you blow.

596
The Oscar statue is the world's most expensive gold-plated dildo.

597
Formal education is a rather helpful but pallid substitute for hardcore experience.

598
Society is being educated by the government, and people wonder where we've gone wrong.

599
Unfortunately, my friend went from Marine Corps to Marine corpse.

600
Weapons, guts, knowledge, and unity combined are the antidote to tyranny.

601
Beware the Ides of March, and the snide of the rest of the year.

602
The only real difference between politicians of any party is how they go about plundering and oppressing we the people.

603
You pissed off the wrong vindictive psychopath!

604
Be passionately objective.

605
Haters hate themselves.

606
A past life reading is like a drive-through anamnesis.

607
Most medical doctors are nothing more than overpaid, glorified prescription writers and licensed drug dealers. I don't take health advice from drug dealers.

608
Times have changed; now there's a sucker born every second.

609
Life is like an invisible rollercoaster, with ups and downs that you can't always see coming.

610
I gave up being a humanitarian. It's much more enjoyable being a raging misanthrope.

611
Have you seen a good person who prospers and is always protected from problems and calamity? Neither have I.

612
Does a mechanical universe necessitate a mechanic?

613
It's a crazy world; Inscape while you can.

614
Criminals are guaranteed a speedy trial and quick release to freedom, while innocent, injured parties often wait interminably for justice and sometimes end up wrongly imprisoned.

615
Justice transpires for those who can afford it.

616
During the scorching summers, to nuke southern Arizona would be redundant.

617
I've paid my dues with compound interest.

618
If you're not yourself, then who are you?

619
May my ex-wife become as corpulent as her rancorous mother.

620
Keep a keen, discerning mind, because an open mind can be filled with erroneous ideas, and a skeptical mind lacks flexibility to perceive the unseen and the seemingly improbable.

621
May my enemy have an out-of-body experience and not return.

622
We wish to live long in good health, but not to grow old and feeble.

623
The woman of my dreams turned into a nightmare.

624
When you're in love with yourself, you'll have few rivals.

625
Idiots never rule; they just think they do.

626
Most businesses succeed by making products designed for planned obsolescence rather than durable quality and ingenuity.

627
The future is created each moment.

628
I'm not superstitious; I'm only super; there's nothing stitious about it.

629
It's a brutal, wicked, depraved, corrupt world. What's your contribution to all this?

630
Fat people should eschew their food.

631
Listening to rappers and current rock bands is preferable to chewing broken glass, but just barely.

632
Nothing will go the way you really want it to, unless you really want it to.

633
Plagiarism is stealing from one or a few sources; research is the robbing of many.

634
Unlike computers, humans cannot delete what they've spoken.

635
Fools do things the herd way.

636
For thousands of years, religion and government are historically proven to be the two most corrupt and pervasive forms of organized crime.

637
If there's a War On Drugs, why are there thousands of drug stores still in business?

638
Where most people's skepticism ends, my intense suspicions continue unabated.

639
Violence is a traditional American pastime ingrained in the national psyche. On television, sex is a sin, but murder is in. Nakedness is banned, but killing is glorified.

640
Give me your tired, your poor, your muddled masses of parasite-ridden scum and deranged, diseased criminals who invade, breed like flies, mooch off welfare, create gangs and slums, sell drugs to children, commit drive-by shootings, and have no interest in our culture.

641
Worrying is like paying a debt one doesn't owe.

642
You know you're not young when you used Yahoo! GeoCities back in the day.

643
Just when you assume that you've mastered a subject, you learn something new about it.

644
Forego the status quo.

645
I haven't killed all of my enemies in cold blood, but I have delighted in hearing of their misfortunes, humiliations, sufferings, and untimely deaths.

646
Who controls information flow controls humanity.

647
Certainty precedes the unforeseen.

648
Do unto the system what it has done unto you.

649
Many self-made men never complete the job.

650
Congressional salary is fossil fuel.

651
These days, too many judges are black-robed dictators.

652
'Tis better to be a wine snob than a beer slob.

653
Many babies are born bright. They gravitate towards intellectual atrophy by aping their daft elders.

654
A banned book is something dangerous to the self-interests of those who ban it.

655
The four most dangerous people in the world are the serious, the cornered coward, the genocidal maniac, and the relentless, hungry salesperson or telemarketer who won't take 'no' for an answer.

656
Invoke happiness and have wild sex often. Such laudable recourse brings no remorse.

657
Slaughtering Natives and stealing their land is an American heritage.

658
All murderous dictators of corrupt regimes agree: gun control works.

659
If I took diet advice from every out-of-shape, fat person, I'd look like them.

660
Do you know why most lottery winners soon end up broke? Because they're not the sharpest tools in the shed.

661
Many people suffered and perished so that you might have the freedom to be an obedient, conformist, brainwashed, shithead sheeple slave like so many other fools.

662
There's nothing wrong with stupid people that extinction won't remedy.

663
It may be Intelligent Design, but it's not necessarily benevolent.

664
Benny Hill was born a commoner, but he became the emperor of comedy.

665
The concept of Maya might be an illusion.

666
Verminous celebrities who have catamites are being exposed into the light.

667
Tattoos are for shallow attention whores who are only skin-deep.

668
How much wisdom has died out from want of worthy successors?

669
Make your own life your favorite reality show.

670
Transform yourself and you will help transform the world.

671
Small talk is for small minds.

672
Sigmund Freud was Sickman Fraud.

673
Do you want magic moments in your life? Then create them.

674
Standardized tests are for standardized minds.

675
Loyalty is the most important trait a person can possess. Loyalty is far more valuable than talent, intellectual prowess, worldly achievements, personality, social status, accumulated wealth, academic degrees, religious beliefs, or physical appearance.

676
When the Cause is Just, the War is Sacred.

677
Protect yourself by protecting your life force energy.

678
When someone pisses you off, simply tell them, "Crawl back into the sewer from where you originated."

679
Climate change happens four times a year: spring, summer, autumn, and winter. Even Vivaldi knew this.

680
We are still in a Dark Age because most people are blind to truths.

681
If you subscribe to the theory of creation, then why didn't your creator give you an owner's manual for your mind?

682
You cannot possibly please everyone, but you can take exquisite and even perverse delight in offending, mocking and punching as many stupid assholes as possible.

683
Everyone is entitled to their own opinions, but only if they agree with me.

684
If MMA is so effective, why does one MMA fighter always lose every bout?

685
Fake meat is lab-concocted crap for fake people who are full of crap.

686
History is living proof that most people don't learn from history.

687
If perseverance and raging anger were athletic events, my neck would be draped with gold medals.

688
Free your mind, and your body will follow.

689
It's what the average person doesn't know that makes them the average person.

690
One doesn't have to be of low I.Q. to rap, but it certainly helps.

691
I'm not impatient; I'm just fed up with waiting.

692
God must love morons; he made so many of them.

693
If like attracts like, why do opposites attract?

694
Who posed for all the different-looking portraits of Christ, why do they all have bizarre forked beards, and why does he look like a White man from Northern Europe?

695
We live, on average, less than a century and spend one-third of it asleep. What a rip-off.

696
I'm not addicted. I just can't quit.

697
I'm a Groucho Marxist and John Lennonist.

698
Join Placebo Addicts Anonymous.

699
I wouldn't sell them the sweat molecules attached to my anal vapors.

700
There are some days when I really don't want to go to work; these days are always every weekend as well as Mondays through Fridays.

701
Those who are bored are boring.

702
Most people rarely discuss or debate to arrive at truth; they only argue to ardently defend their cherished Belief System, which abbreviated is B.S.

703
Free love has a high price.

704
The media is a weapon of crass deception.

705
Once you become your own boss, there is no turning back to being a mere employee.

706
No socialist or communist in any Western country wants to be shipped permanently to Venezuela or North Korea, because these leftists don't want a harsh reality check.

707
Extension of life does not necessarily provide quality of life.

708
I love wisdom far more than I love my ex-girlfriend, because she left me, and wisdom did not.

709
How many functioning brain cells does it take to be a music or movie critic?

710
Take good care of your body when you're young, and it can take good care of you when you're older.

711
Tobacco companies should be immune from liability lawsuits; if smokers are dumb enough to continually inhale carcinogenic, toxic, stinking fumes by their own volition, they get what they deserve.

712
The word 'belief' contains the word 'lie'.

713
Calling something 'deluxe' is admitting that it's entirely mediocre.

714
If the mainstream media is the measure of national intelligence, then this is a nation of blithering fools.

715
Patience is a virtue up to a certain point, after which it becomes a serious liability.

716
Most modern music should have never been written nor recorded.

717
Lifting weights helps you lose weight.

718
Fame isn't for everyone. That's why not everyone is famous.

719
I neither forgive nor forget.

720
I've tolerated the intolerable; now what do I do?

721
Ninety-nine percent of history is not written.

722
What you assume you excel at, somewhere there is an Asian child doing it just as well or far better.

723
I'm not against all laws, just bad ones.

724
'Work' is the most profane four-letter word.

725
The Battle Hymn of the Republic has morphed into the Babble Him of the Repugnant.

726
Economic slavery is a thriving global industry.

727
It's not easy raising one's parents. For one thing, I didn't spank mine nearly enough.

728
Beware of Greeks bearing scriptures.

729
Do you want to evolve? Then stop being stupid.

730
The government taxes our patience.

731
99% of all movies and television shows are colossal wastes of one's time, money, and consciousness.

732
Get a tattoo to express your unique individualism and stand out from the crowds–just like all the other millions of idiot clones that did the exact same thing.

733
I never watch horror films. For horror of the worst kind, I watch the evening news or read the Old Testament.

734
God created man in his own image; after that, no wonder things went wrong.

735
Opinions are indeed like assholes; most of them stink because they're full of shit.

736
With so much work to do, I don't have time to apply for unemployment welfare benefits.

737
I believe in UFOs, as I've seen several flying objects that were clearly unidentified.

738
I believe in aliens! Millions of them have invaded my country, and my taxes pay for their free welfare and criminal actions.

739
The best thing about the present moment is that it isn't the past. Yet.

740
God never gives anyone more problems or burdens than they can handle–except for all the people who were driven to suicide.

741
I'm terribly cruel and vindictive, but only to those who deserve it.

742
Many politicians make excellent gravediggers; after all, they're hard at work digging graves for their countries.

743
Screw unto others as they screw unto you.

744
For someone who's taken a vow of poverty, the pope lives in quite the slum hovel.

745
Think outside the box? What box?

746
Some people's torrents of negativity resemble an overflowing toilet.

747
Reality is an optical illusion.

748
Acting is the easiest job in the world. Where else can one make multiple mistakes and still get another take without being fired?

749
This country is the fascist growing nation on earth.

750
Music used to soothe the savage beast; now it creates them.

751
How do you know that Rome wasn't built in a day? You weren't there.

752
I detest driving behind someone who has no place to go and all day to get there.

753
Oxygen thieves clog the freeways like plaque in an artery.

754
Home is where the hearth is.

755
I brake for tsunamis.

756
Lose weight now! Stop bending your elbows.

757
Scientific studies show that ten out of ten people are afflicted with stupidity due to a lack of intelligence.

758
Most people struggle through life working lousy, dead-end jobs they detest just so they can finance their misery.

759
Scrooge was right: Christmas is a sham.

760
Wisdom is said to be of high value, but no creditor accepts aphorisms in lieu of monetary payments.

761
The road to success is anything but a smooth ride.

762
Since World War II, the U.S. military hasn't won a war, but it has started many of them. Winning wars is no longer the goal, because protracting wars is far more profitable.

763
The halls of justice have become the temples of tyranny.

764
No matter where humans go, there they pollute.

765
How does one distinguish Divine Will from Cause and Effect?

766
One (shitty) day at a time.

767
Equality is a misnomer. One cannot make stupid, lazy people equal with smart, productive people, and expect society to be balanced and flourish.

768
Who audits tax collectors?

769
Who polices the police?

770
Who judges the judges?

771
Who regulates the regulators?

772
Who legislates the legislators?

773
Who rules the rulers?

774
Who tyrannizes tyrants?

775
Censorship is the left hand of dictatorship.

776
The most effective means of completely eroding freedom is to gradually, incrementally make oppression not only acceptable, but urgently needed, and even fashionable.

777
Forgiveness is for weaklings too cowardly to exact revenge.

778
In life, some people burn bridges and move on. Not me. I don't burn bridges; I rig them with high explosives and cordially invite my enemies to cross them.

779
No one should consume any psychoactive drugs until they are physically, emotionally, mentally, and spiritually prepared through training by experienced, enlightened mentors.

780
Most strangers are just dysfunctional, toxic, stupid losers that you haven't met yet and don't want to know.

781
There's a reason why the stout and sturdy Yeomen Warders are known as Beefeaters, not as vegan grazers.

782
The law of Survival of the Fittest was never made void by civilization's jurisprudence.

783
Instead of settling for being an ignorant, gullible consumer, be an intelligent, well-informed citizen.

784
Use your head for something besides being an ornament.

785
There's no law against being stupid. There should be.

786
Death is Nature's way of telling you to slow down and take it easy.

787
Killing one's enemies is not wrong, it's merely illegal in most jurisdictions.

788
Occam's razor is perpetually sharp.

789
Great minds create. Petty minds criticize.

790
When you eat your food, it goes to waist.
When you throw it away, it goes to waste.

791
I only associate with the affluent, not the effluent.

792
Loyal, genuine friends are so valuable, that they cannot be purchased at any price.

793
My Special Theory of Relativism is this: never do business with relatives. They're usually a pain in the assets.

794
The individual act of disobedience to tyrannical authority and its oppressive laws are a prerequisite to staging a usurpation of oppression.

795
American pride goes before a fall.

796
Our leaders speak with such eloquent double-talk; well, most of them do.

797
For your safety and security, we're working towards a tougher, more evil dictatorship.

798
How easily sheeple surrender their dwindling freedoms for the promised security of a gilded cage.

799
It's easy to turn from good to evil, but difficult to return to good.

800
Laws written by tyrants are nothing but pieces of paper to be torn into shreds—after the tyrants are deposed and disposed.

801
The most powerful tool of tyranny is ignorance.

802
What a lovely day for extirpating psychopathic totalitarians.

803
If I seem to be cynical, it's because I am.

804
The older I get, the more I can't stand almost all people.

805
The largest paradigm shift is happening now. Embrace it or deny, but you cannot stop it.

806
I don't get mad, and I don't get even. I get silent, and I get revenge!

807
It's good to be egotistical, because no one else will do that for you.

808
One cannot make a living providing free platitudes to the multitudes; that's why I charge money for mine.

809
Never judge anyone by their appearance, but absolutely judge them by their words, attitudes, and actions.

810
People generally fall in love when they're young and fresh, because it's not easy falling in love with a wrinkled, sagging, unattractive, decrepit, smelly old fart.

811
It is exasperating being a profound genius surrounded by superficial idiots.

812
I intend to die with plenty of happy memories, not unfulfilled dreams.

813
I want to read the banned books, peruse the destroyed manuscripts, study the censored videos and websites, read the prohibited blogs, newspapers and magazine articles, hear the advice and stories of the wise who are ignored by the media, see the quashed evidence, and possess the suppressed technologies. Only until then will I have a shred of hope to find some truth.

814
Shift has hit the fan blades of change. Either take a big Shift or be full of Shift. Either way, Shift into higher spiritual gear, smoke some good Shift, become a total Shift-head, and then you'll give a Shift as you exclaim, "Why is this Shift happening to me?" Because Shift happens, and it's good to be in deep Shift. And, if people don't like this, I don't give a Shift!

815
Learn from the past, apply to the present, and create your future.

816
The good news about death is that it will permanently end all of your problems.

817
Whether you like it or not, the future is coming. Prepare for it.

818
It's me against the world, and the odds are decidedly in my favor.

819
Hardly anyone knows beforehand the time of their death, but everyone can choose the moment of their enlightenment.

820
Those who are excluded from Self Mastery, exclude themselves.

821
With caffeine, almost all things are possible.

822
Brainwashing is good when you wash your own brain.

823
As pride goes before a fall, gratitude precedes greatness.

824
Increase your perceptive abilities, expand your consciousness, evolve your awareness.

825
Rock music used to be dangerous; now it's a corpse in need of a proper burial.

826
There is no Third World; there is only One World.

827
To inspire the future, delve into the past.

828
The most difficult challenges don't necessarily always bring the promised rewards; too often, they're just shitty experiences that were never needed, desired, prayed for or deserved.

829
The number of humans embracing woke ideology is proof that many peasants are easily fooled.

830
Your ancestors want you to succeed and prosper. They are cheering for you. So am I.

831
It's not just mind over matter, it's mind *in* matter, and matter doesn't mind at all.

832
Fill your heart with truth, compassion, and zeal for righteousness, and none of it will matter.

833
Once you see and accept the truth, you cannot 'un-see' and reject it (unless you're really stupid).

834
If you let a Hell Being take over your life, it will turn your life into a hell.

835
To be human is to be astoundingly brave. Gods and demons are beings too cowardly to be humans.

836
Instead of building weapons of mass destruction, let's embrace methods of mass illumination.

837
Nihilism is a belief for people too cowardly to commit suicide.

838
Hypnotic hip tonic.

839
The longer I'm still alive, the more abhorrence I have for the majority of homo sapiens.

840
We've had it all backwards for too long. Young people should be the ones who vote for war, and send the old politicians off to fight and die, while we stay home, get drunk, get high, and get laid!

841
I make Scrooge look like a flaming spendthrift philanthropist.

842
Being highly intelligent is sometimes aggravating, because one is forced to severely dumb down their conversations to the level of an imbecile in order to interact with average people.

843
When you entertain an idiot, you become part of their stupidity.

844
If you desire power over others, first master yourself.

845
Deep cultivation of one's self is destined to blossom and bear fruit.

846
Why escape reality when you can create it?

847
Temptation comes in several guises and flavors.

848
Vanity demands incessant external validation.

849
I'm a staunch antiauthoritarian, but only when I'm not allowed to be the authority.

850
Revolution is the removal of the archaic.

851
He was a perfidious, posing, pretentious, penurious, parasite poof peddling potentially puerile, paltry pipe dreams perpetually promoting pessimism, provocation, and prosaicism.

852
The USA is the land of excessive litigation; a utopia for shysters and greedy plaintiffs.

853
Pretentious Talking Head
With voice quite absurd
Obnoxious inflection
Please, don't say a word!

854
Life is what you fake it,
at least until you make it.
Then you gotta shake it,
and possibly remake it.

855
I came to this conclusion
as I sat upon my throne:
a royal without subjects
is left to rule alone.

856
Some people take a vow of poverty.
I've taken a vow of luxury.
Some people take a vow of chastity.
I've taken a vow of lust fulfillment.
Some people take a vow of silence.
I've taken a vow of scintillating conversation and screaming orgasms.
Some people take a vow to live in the middle of nowhere.
I've taken a vow to live on the edge of somewhere.

857
Moments turn into minutes.
Minutes turn into hours.
Hours turn into days.
Days turn into weeks.
Weeks turn into months.
Months turn into years.
Years turn into decades.
Decades turn into your life.
Live in the moment.

Relationships

858
Give a woman an inch, and she'll desire eight more.

859
A man cannot serve two masters, but he can serve as many mistresses as he can afford.

860
I didn't need to break a mirror to get seven years of bad luck; instead, I got married.

861
I asked for her hand in marriage, and she replied, "Why not ask for the rest of my body as well?"

862
Most every woman's favorite five words from every man are, "I'll buy it for you!"

863
Many physically beautiful people are the opposite in character.

864
When you choose a partner for marriage, cohabiting, or just sex, remember that eventually lust expires. Then what?

865
My ex-girlfriend enjoyed bickering and arguing; it broke up the monotony of a perfectly happy relationship.

866
When it comes to sex partners, I'm not picky–most any pair of stunningly beautiful, young nymphomaniacs will do.

867
Many men may think a woman is beautiful until they see her other face.

868
Marriage is like a ship: courtship, relationship, hardship.

869
My wife gave me an ultimatum: choose her or my mistress, but I can't have both.
I don't miss my wife at all.

870
My friend lost 199 pounds of ugly fat in one day.
He got a divorce from his American wife.

871
Have a monogamous relationship with yourself.

872
Beside every successful, happily-married man is a loving, wonderful wife.

873
I was in a same-sex marriage: it was the same sex with the same boring wife.

874
I charge premium prices for giving my attention to women. I take cash, gold, silver, platinum, gems, checks, money orders, credit and debit cards, cryptocurrency, and titles to unencumbered assets worth owning.

875
99.9% of all heterosexual women are turned on if a man says this: "In addition to being devastatingly handsome and tall, I'm wealthy, funny and am hugely endowed!"

876
Today I met my future wife, and she is why I will remain single.

877
You've heard of the seven-year itch? With my last wife, I had that itch after only seven days.

878
I would give up having wild sex with gorgeous, slutty teenage girls, except that I don't want to!

879
I'm a member of planned parenthood: I plan to avoid parenthood and single mothers.

880
The difference between a whore and a gold digger is that, unlike the gold digger, the whore is upfront and honest about her intent from the start, and she's not nearly as expensive.

881
Why do women get makeovers? Because so many of them are unattractive.

882
Today, marriage is often a mutual convenience merger with a planned exit strategy.

883
A lot of men are like lightbulbs: when they get dim or go out, they are easily replaced.

884
I like women as I like eggs: they used to be scrambled and deviled. Then, for a while, they were over easy and sunny side up. Now they're young and raw. And the yolk is on me.

885
One man's trash is another man's wife.

886
I wanted to get married in the worst way, and I did—in the *worst* way.

887
She wanted to put a ring on my finger, and I gave her the finger alright!

888
I only like two types of women: young and beautiful.

889
I desire a girlfriend who can both defy and define entropy.

890
It is better to have loved and lost than to be shackled to a psychotic spouse for the rest of your miserable life.

891
Never, ever waste an erection!

892
They say sex sells, but I'm renting, not buying it.

893
I always cry at weddings, because I know what awaits the hapless groom.

894
It's no coincidence that 'wife' rhymes with 'strife', and 'husband' is eerily similar to 'housebound'.

895
My wife and I were two ships passing water in the night.

896
It's better to shag a successful 'career woman' than to be manacled in matrimony to a shallow gold digger.

897
The only pleasure he ever gave his wife was the act of paying her alimony.

898
His wife calls him 'Minute Man'–that's how long he lasts in bed.

899
I love you to death, and the sooner, the better.

900
I don't want to get married unless my wife is an ostentatiously rich, young, stunningly beautiful sex addict who's too proud to have her husband work.

901
The freedom from a bad marriage is beyond price.

902
I want a bent bint.

903
I am vigorously practicing polyamory with several beautiful, young, naughty ladies until I get it right.

904
Marriage is a book. The first chapter is a fairy tale, and the rest of it is a nightmare novel from hell.

Comedy

905
They told me, "Start your free trial today!" I told them I don't want to be put on trial, even if it is free.

906
Occasionally I like to mess with clueless people's heads by asking them, "How many days does it take for the sun to circumnavigate the earth?"

907
My wife turned into a nun. When it came to sex and happiness, there was nun to be had.

908
Have you ever wondered how porcupines have sex? It's got to be a sticky situation with a lot of pricks!

909
They say repetition is the mother of all skills. I don't know who the father of all skills is, but he must be liable for a massive amount of child support payments.

910
The optimist says the glass is half full. The pessimist says it's half empty. The realistic says it's totally full of both liquid and air. I say I want to know what's in it, and after I drink it, can I get free refills?

911
We have smart phones, smart cars, smart homes, smart appliances, smart locks, smart thermostats, smart doorbells, smart watches, smart bands, smart keychains, smart speakers, smart cameras, and now even smart toilets–all for a teeming herd of boors.

912
LOL stands for Loser Obviously Lacking.

913
If I had a dollar for every idiot on this planet, I'd be a multi-billionaire.

914
I would play golf except that I lack the enthusiasm and proclivity to take a long stick and hit one of my balls in public.

915
At my age, I still have a lot of love to give, but I now charge by the inch and by the hour.

916
Too often, I want to ask certain people, "Were you born this way, or did you make a determined effort to become a stupid a-hole?"

917
I don't call it licking the bowl or plate clean; I refer to it as making oral love to the last of the sauce. How's that for a visual?

918
Don't call me a lazy couch potato. I'm a sedentary sofa spud.

919
I met an English girl who was so stunningly beautiful, that I wanted to stick my Cockney in her Anglo and have wild Saxon with her!

920
During a job interview, they asked me if I'd be willing to submit to a drug test, and I replied, "That depends on what kind of drugs you want me to test."

921
I've lived all alone for years now after I lost my wife, and I hope to never find her.

922
The Internet has allowed people from all over the world to come together, especially when watching porn.

923
If a comedian can't write their own material, they're not a real comedian. They're a joke.

924
Drum machines suck! And so do vacuums.

925
Heaven's streets are indeed paved with 24 karat gold, and I'm stripping the gold off the streets faster than they can repave them!

926
Most humans aren't even worthy of my flatulence, but in some people's cases, I make exceptions!

927
Yes, I fondly remember the 1990s, back when talented people actually used to win music awards.

928
I can have sex for hours, and usually it's with a partner or two.

929
Ever since I reached puberty, I've been battling a severe weight problem: evading the sexual advances of obese females.

930
As a mature man, the older I get, the more I miss the simple things I had as a little kid, like fattening snacks, naptime, and spankings on heavily-padded diapers.

931
If it weren't for clothing, we'd have to see hideously ugly naked bodies everywhere. Thank goodness for the makers and sellers of these textiles to cover people!

932
The straight and narrow path sucks! I prefer the curvy, broad, and easy way paved in gold and lined with free food, quality drugs, and affordable hookers.

933
I learnt to play the guitar by ear. After that, I switched to using my fingers. That's why I don't 'ear too well.

934
Modern sexology studies show that most men last only one or two minutes before either ejaculating or losing their erections. This has created the biggest problem in the world: most women are sexually frustrated!

935
I'm glad that more women are participating in sports previously exclusive to males, but I draw the line at watching female sumo wrestlers, lest I lose my lunch.

936
It's no coincidence that the word 'psychotherapist' is 'psycho the rapist'. I'm not going anywhere near anyone who calls themselves that!

937
In January 2021, a survey claimed that only 46% of Americans still trust the mainstream media, so almost half the population are gullible shitheads.

938
Somewhere, there is a woman giving birth to a toxic narcissist every six seconds. She must be found and stopped!

939
We're all God's children; it's just that more than a few should have been aborted.

940
I support equality for all nine, or seventeen, or twenty-three, or seven hundred and seventy-seven, or however many genders there are this week.

941
My doctor told me that I have psychosis of the liver. I had no idea it was that bad.

942
My doctor also warned me to give up all alcohol and marijuana to avoid brain damage. I replied, "My brain is fine, so there's no reason to stop smoking booze or drinking pot."

943
I know a man who would be a complete asshole, except that some parts are missing.

944
People are always shocked when I tell them my age, as they say I look decades younger. I tell them it's because I'm only as old as the young ladies I feel.

945
Not that I'm complaining, but I had a severe case of Reverse Erectile Dysfunction: it didn't know when to stop functioning.

946
At the rate of progressive insanity, soon we'll be encountering humanoids claiming to be multi-species, LGBTQAAA+++--&#@, non-binary, non-trinary, non-quadinary, gender-fluid, body fluid, brake fluid, transgendered, transnational, interdimensional, insectoid alien, computer, nano-technology virus, invisible entities with absolutely no pronouns! Try putting that on a name tag!

947
I am so looking forward to when the easily-offended snowflake generation gets old and decrepit, and they're shocked and horrified at the young generations who are blunt, obscenely rude, and mean-spirited at them.

948
Due to political correctness, childhood is now required to be childproof.

949
I'm like Jesus: he turned water into wine, and I can turn wine into passing water.

950
Breaking news! God embraces atheism!

951
Communism has only one joke: Why did the bourgeois cross the road? To oppress the proletariat, of course. Why else?

952
I told my astrologer, "If you don't stop yammering indecipherable astrological jargon, I'm gonna shove my Venus up Uranus!"

953
He's not fat; he's just got extensively expansive adiposity.

954
A decade ago, I rapidly lost all body fat on the Southern California Special Diet: per day, it's one small meal, plenty of water to stay hydrated, and twelve large lines of pure uncut Nose Candy.

955
It's too late to apologize, but I will accept all of your assets and your spawn to sell as chattel.

956
He was such a loser that he finally broke down and offered to sell his soul to Satan, but even Satan declined him.

957
Whenever I want to impress an intelligent woman, I unzip my personal notebook, whip out my colossal lexicon, and proudly show her my magnificent dangling participle.

958
Peeing and a good bowel movement are two of life's simple pleasures.

959
Wi-Fi isn't offered at many religious buildings because they cannot compete with an invisible power that actually works reliably.

960
Forget the Big Bang Theory. The universe was created by the Big Bong.

961
Back in the 2000s decade, I tried emailing her a penis picture, but her Inbox wasn't large enough to handle the size of my file.

962
I hear your indolent wife has a big lump growing on her body. Now she knows how her couch feels.

963
Losers of the world, unite! And then off yourselves.

964
Different strokes for different folks, particularly when wanking.

965
I'm so dyslexic that I swear my doctor said that I'm blind in one ear, and deaf in my left eye.

966
I know a man who's so full of his own shit, that if he grew two more assholes, he could start a global fertilizer company.

967
I met a Native American medicine man who was a true tea connoisseur; he drank so much tea, he drowned in his tea pee.

968
An American man went all the way to the U.K. to buy a fanny pack, and he ended up with a pack of fannies, alright.

969
I went through drug rehabilitation: I successfully rehabilitated a lot of good drugs. They're all doing fine now! To show their gratitude, they still keep in touch.

970
While living in Southern California, I applied for disability benefits, as my handicap was a rare case of fluency in English without saying the word 'like' a dozen times per minute.

971
They asked me if I'm an extrovert or an introvert. Apparently "pervert" is the wrong answer.

972
I wanted to get a copy of the *Tightwad Gazette*, but I'm too cheap to pay for it.

973
It's sad that proctologists are the jokes of so many butts.

974
Some people are so obese, they can sink rowing machines.

975
I have a heart of gold. I hate to tell you what my bowels are made of though.

976
My girlfriend worked in construction as a stud finder. That's how she found me.

977
He sold his soul to the devil for manufacturer's suggested retail price bearing interest with a hedged insurance coverage against depreciation, wear and tear, expired warranties, lawsuits, liens, encumbrances, hidden fees, surcharges, retroactive taxes, and a one-year money back guarantee if not completely satisfied.

978
Christian: "Have you found the Lord?"
Me: "Why? Have you lost him again?"

979
My dysfunctional Christian parents drove me to drink, drugs, and fornication–and I never had the courtesy to thank them.

980
No wonder we humans are so messed up–right after we're born, we get assaulted by a spanking, and we haven't even done anything wrong yet!

981
Some critics claim that marijuana causes depression, and I agree; when I run out of marijuana, I always get depressed!

982
Several years ago, when someone first told me about Instagram, I thought it was a cocaine delivery service, so I did an internet search for Instakilo.

983
I don't have a problem with porn. I enjoy profiting from it–no problem!

984
My girlfriend gets turned on when I engage in S & M: Sweeping & Mopping. Meanwhile, she likes BDSM: Buying Damn Stuff Manically.

985
Americans spend over $700 million every year on over-the-counter laxatives. This is irrefutable proof that many of them are completely full of their own shit.

986
Independent studies show that the most shocking tactic to deal with someone who incessantly engages in gaslighting you is to, without warning, douse them with gasoline and light them on fire. Scientific experiments show it works every time.

987
My nice Jewish neighbor kid said he attends a 'sinner-gog' on Shabbat.

988
I once saw a man bludgeoning and burning the ground. I guess that's what they call 'beating a path' and 'blazing a trail'.

989
When speaking modern West Coast Americanese, remember the syntactical rule that the random word 'like' precedes a minimum of every three words spoken sequentially.

990
It's been said that the body is a temple, and many Americans' bodies have room to spare for an entire congregation.

991
Women can do everything that men can do, except play with their balls and ejaculate semen through a penis.

992
The girls I fancy most are like olive oil: they're extra virgin.

993
I do not have xenophobia. I'm not afraid of any xeno. I don't even know what a fucking xeno is, so how can I be afraid of it?

994
It's not illegal dumping; it's giving back to the community.

995
For the self-indulgent Baby Boomers, it used to be sex, drugs, and rock & roll. Now it's impotence, meds, and adult diapers.

996
As an ugly tranny, he's the kind of woman that no man wants.

997
Some standup comedians should remain seated.

998
A cider factory was robbed of most of its cider. Officials believe it was an in-cider job.

999
My father told me, "You're not a spring chicken anymore."
I replied, "True. Now I'm a late summer cock."

1,000
I make documentary videos and romantic movies for men. Some people call them 'Adult Entertainment'.

1,001
My psychiatrist diagnosed me as a psychopathic maniac. He was *obviously* wrong, so I grabbed an axe, chopped him up, and fed him to my mastiff.

1,002
She's like the typical girl next door…if you're living next to a pig pen.

1,003
William Shakespeare liked marijuana. After all, one of his most famous quotes is "Doobie or not doobie? That is the question." And the answer is "Doobie"!

1,004
My ex-mother-in-law reminded me of a Long Island Ice Tea: tall, cold, and full of booze.

1,005
Heterosexual alpha males who enjoy cigars are an odd lot. Any man who delights in sucking on a penis-shaped object probably has gay issues.

1,006
I support feminists, but only those who are young, beautiful, generously buy me dinners at fancy restaurants, and enthusiastically have sex with me. After all, I have standards, too.

1,007
I was single and abstained from sex for fifteen long years! Then I turned sixteen and said, "Enough of that! Time to get laid!"

1,008
I'm old enough to know that the '#' symbol is called a 'pound sign', so when I see #metoo, I can't help but automatically read it as 'Pound me too!'

1,009
I love my country, but I dislike a sizable percentage of its inhabitants.

1,010
It's only funny until someone gets seriously injured or dies–and then it's hilarious!

1,011
Here's a bumper sticker you never see: "My child is an aborted fetus kept in a jar!"

1,012
When it comes to texting, I'm all thumbs.

1,013
My pet rock is smarter than many humans.

My Gift Wish List

1,014
Peace on Earth, or at least everywhere I happen to be.

1,015
Inflatable life-size replica of the Great Wall of China.

1,016
Super Hero outfit with anti-gravity boots, mauve-embroidered 3-D cape, and gem-encrusted helmet.

1,017
Black 1999 Lamborghini Diablo autographed by Attila the Hun, Mata Hari, and any cartoon character.

1,018
40-foot length shipping container filled to the brim with serendipity and $50 Trillion in cash and precious metals.

1,019
Vat of vintage Martian wine made from organic gooseberries and neutrino-infused stardust.

1,020
The steering wheel, warning bell, chandelier, and two propeller blades from the RMS Titanic.

1,021
Eternal ecstasy served on a gold platter with built-in yodeling music box, ATM, and teleporter module.

1,022
Artificial Intelligence powered by genuine altruism, and a self-destruct button in case of an emergency.

1,023
A one-year holiday to a parallel universe, because when you've seen one galaxy here, you've seen them all.

1,024
Verisimilitude in the media and politics.

1,025
Elder Runes-engraved magic wand/laser pointer/hand buzzer made by an unruly Icelandic elf queen.

1,026
A Hi-Fi sound system loud enough to be heard with clarity on the Dark Side of the Moon.

1,027
Authentic succour.

1,028
The unused portion of a fake news anchor's brain.

1,029
Glow-in-the-dark, nuclear-powered golf club with auto-site Aim & Fire, and detachable whiskey flask.

1,030
369 cubic acres of prime oceanfront property in either Atlantis, Lemuria, or a land-locked country.

1,031
The ability to think parenthetically (but not always).

1,032
Mother Theresa's snuffbox, Colt .45 handgun, and Death Metal record collection.

1,033
Edible radioactive isotopes shaped like gummy bears, tacos, sushi rolls, and live ammo.

1,034
Holographic pop-up book *'The Gulag Internment of Psychopathic Autocrats"*.

1,035
Reverse-polarity mirror made by a Sumerian shaman scribe fluent in Sanskrit, Swahili, and semaphore.

1,036
A 1/100,000th scale model of the Sun (batteries not included).

1,037
Autographed 1ˢᵗ Edition of 'The Kardashian's Complete Guide to Quantum Physics, Superstring Theory, Time Travel, Applied Keynesian Economics, and Tapeworm-Induced Personality Disorders'.

1,038
Centaur with purple stripes, cloven hooves, dreadlocks mane, and an ancient Albanian accent.

1,039
A bottle of twaddle.

1,040
120 pounds of precisely what I'm desiring.

1,041
Solar-powered cellphone with ring tone of a screaming orgasm during a harpsichord recital in a medieval dungeon.

1,042
The Washington Monument painted in neon pink and yellow polka-dots during a leap year.

1,043
Lilac-scented grab bag of unused metaphors.

1,044
Two nuns wearing tight yoga pants, pushup bras, sexy stilettos, blue lipstick, and brass knuckles.

1,045
A four-and-a-half leaf clover.

1,046
A backpack of toy tactical mini-nukes (for Ages 5 and Up; parental supervision optional).

1,047
Commemorative Full-Color Tour Guide *'Bigfoot's Penthouse & Secret Military Bases That Don't Exist'*.

1,048
Pocket-size, remote control supercollider.

1,049
One gallon of mirth.

1,050
Over-the-counter, do-it-yourself combo Brain Surgery and Stomach Stapling kit.

1,051
A 10,000-watt electric tuba adorned with rare-earth elements from Austria, Taiwan, and Neptune.

1,052
A guest pass to an outdoor tanning salon in Antarctica.

1,053
Genius without ignominy.

1,054
A fresh flight attendant and her cockpit.

1,055
Complete Braille Anthology of Somalian Pirate Sea Shanties in the keys of F flat and B sharp.

1,056
An internationally-staffed harem with skills in gourmet cuisine, therapeutic massage, belly dancing, abacus calculating, and sharpshooting.

1,057
A suitcase of incongruent anomalies and obscene *non sequiturs*.

1,058
Combination device of a wrist sundial, inter-dimensional telescope, and cannabis vape pen holder.

1,059
A 5-milliliter vial of Great White Shark earwax certified by Prince Valiant and a Uruguayan taxi driver.

1,060
More than enough validation.

1,061
A sacred cow or a sacrilegious goat.

1,062
One large martini glass of mead and suffering succotash–shaken not stirred.

1,063
Children's 8K 3D video *'Ultimate Tag-Team Fight Match: Bambi & The Teletubbies Versus Darth Vader & Godzilla'*.

1,064
A free lifetime supply of assorted, cherry-flavored sublingual synchronicities.

1,065
And something unique and unusual…

Random Questions People Have Asked Me

Below are a series of random questions people have asked me over the years, and my answers.

Q: Are you a virgin?
A: Yes. I admit I've been a virgin twice, and am keenly looking forward to the third time which is supposed to be the charm.

Q: How tall are you?
A: It varies between five feet thirteen inches and six feet one inch, and even occasionally reaches 185.45 cm!

Q: When and where were you born?
A: A long time ago in a galaxy far, far away...

Q: When you were young, what was your dream job?
A: I dreamt of being rich, not having a job.

Q: Do you smoke?
A: Only when on fire.

Q: What was the last State you visited?
A: The State of Bliss, which is far preferable to the State of Insanity.

Q: Have you ever tried bungee jumping?
A: Yes, but without that pesky stretchy cord thingy that gets in the way.

Q: Are you realistic?
A: I'm also surrealistic.

Q: In your writing and speech, do you employ metaphors and allegories?
A: No, I have my all metaphors and allegories work for free, and contractually prohibit them from forming a labor union and going on strike.

Q: What body part do you dislike the most?
A: Spleen cell number 16,374 that died eleven years and three months ago after it vituperatively went on a hunger strike for no good reason.

Q: What body part do you wash first?
A: Crown chakra.

Q: What body part do you wash last?
A: Gall bladder. It takes a lot of gall.

Q: Describe your favorite book in one word.
A: Dilapidated.

Q: Describe the plot of a well-known movie using only four words.
A: Titanic sunk. Big deal.

Q: What is your favorite film?
A: *Life of Brian*.

Q: What is your favorite color?
A: YINMN Blue.

Q: Do you get upset when you don't get to see an episode of your favorite reality TV show?
A: There's a free reality show on 24/7. It's called Life. Get one.

Q: Do you sing in the shower?
A: Usually in the shower, I vape consecrated marijuana concentrates, drink chilled Han Jan Soju neat, recite classical orations from World literature, play the bongos, roll on the floor and speak in tongues, beat my chest, howl, cut myself in blood sacrifices, and scream pagan war songs of my berserker ancestors while having wild sex with beautiful twin nymphomaniacs. But I do *not* sing in the shower, because that would be, well, silly!

Q: What was your first concert?
A: Electric oboe quartet playing death metal lullabies in the keys of E Sharp and Z Flat.

Q: Do you have any pets?
A: Yes, three of them:
   1. a fire-breathing, multi-lingual, spotted blue Unicorn that holds a pilot's license valid in Paraguay, Rhodesia, the Seychelle Islands, and a small moon near Jupiter.

   2. the Sphinx's twin, and

3. a charming, potty-trained Tyrannosaurus Rex that can act, sing, dance, tell jokes, and nimbly play the xylophone at parties, weddings, bar mitzvahs, baptisms, baby showers, strip clubs, and brothels.

Q: Describe your house in one word.
A: Private.

Q: Describe your personal style in one word.
A: Superlative.

Q: Describe your emotions in one word.
A: Intense.

Q: Describe your actions in one word.
A: Unpredictable.

Q: Describe your thinking in one word.
A: Mysterious.

Q: Describe yourself in one word.
A: Ineffable.

Q: Have you ever played air guitar?
A: Yes, and I also played air kazoo, air tuba, air alphorn, and my Derry air.

Q: How many drinks does it take to get you drunk?
A: I'm not a cheap date. I have an extremely high tolerance beyond most anyone you've ever met, but that's okay, because I don't drink alcohol anymore (except in the shower).

Q: How old are you?
A: Old enough to know better, and young enough to do it for hours.

Q: Are you into acting?
A: Only with impunity.

Q: Are you a food snob?
A: Tis better to be a healthy food snob than an unhealthy fat slob.

Q: Are you an elitist?
A: Yes, I confess I am, especially during High Tea. I associate with the affluent, not the effluent.

Q: Do you have any allergies?
A: Yes, I'm highly allergic to three things: manual labor, stupidity, and bullshit.

Q: If our company had a workplace wellness hour, which of the following would you prefer:
- guided meditation
- nature walk/picnic with the team
- virtual yoga session
- puppy therapy, or
- other?

A: I'd like a guided virtual other puppy yoga picnic therapy session. Not available? Okay, how about a free meal and a paid hour-long nap?

Q: Do you prefer to work for a start-up company or an international company?
A: Already having worked for international companies, I'd much rather *own* a start-up company, and have others work for it, and also invest in select international companies, too.

Q: Would you rather have to listen to only Justin Bieber or only Lil Wayne for the rest of your life?
A: Just kill me now.

Q: Do you prefer living in a big city or in the countryside?
A: Having done both, I prefer a sparsely-populated beach town within yachting distance of a larger coastal city.

Q: Do you prefer living in a treehouse or an igloo?
A: An igloo in the Marshall Islands is far preferable to a treehouse in Point Barrow, Alaska.

Q: What is the last great book you read?
A: *Stomach Stapling, Knitting Needle Lobotomies, Rectal Leeches, Do-It-Yourself Eye & Brain Surgery, and Other Easy Home Remedies* by Izzy Dedyett (23rd Edition).

Q: What is the one common factor that all of your ex's had?
A: They were great in bed. No, wait: they were all crazy. Yes, that's it: fucking mad, they were. The lot.

Q: Are you gay?
A: Only for two minutes every one hundred and thirty-eight years.

Q: Do you have a sexual preference?
A: Yes, I prefer having sex as to not having it, depending on the partners, of course.

Q: Are you into casual sex?
A: Oh yes, casual sex is great, and I also like dress-up formal Black-Tie sex, too.

Q: How many women have you slept with?
A: It's impossible to get any sleep during protracted wild sex and screaming orgasms.

Q: Are you vocal during sex?
A: Usually I'm lead guitar and backing vocal, and also song writer, producer, and exuberant groupie instructor.

Q: Current Crush?
A: She who must not be named.

Q: Did you get plastic surgery?
A: A plastic surgeon promptly altered my face after he caught me kissing his nubile teenage daughter.

Q: Who is your favorite cartoon character?
A: Scrooge McDuck.

Q: Would you rather be a wizard or a superhero?
A: I'm already a wizard.

Q: What makes a superhero the most "powerful"?
A: How many times the 'superhero' blows the movie studio producers *and* the directors.

Q: What is your favorite flavor of ice cream?
A: Persian vanilla ice cream with pistachios, rose water, and saffron.

Q: Have you ever made out in a movie theater?
A: No, but one time in a dark theater, I did receive an amazing blowjob that lasted over forty-five minutes!

Q: What was the worst thing your parents ever grounded you for?
A: In First Grade, using an English medieval axe to chop up a bully classmate, then igniting a micro-sized thermonuclear warhead on the playground—just to see what it would do.

Q: Who is the last person you think about before falling asleep?
A: My lovely, luscious, lusty Asian mistress who sleeps beside me in our extremely large, lavish, luxurious bed.

Q: What do you look for in an intimate relationship?
A: Profound, life-enhancing experiences with a multi-dimensional, highly intelligent, dazzlingly articulate, witty, physically-outstanding carbon-based lifeform infused with a pleasant demeanor, irreverent sense of humor, polyglot abilities, and an exceptional, insatiable naughty streak.

Q: Did you ever abuse drugs?
A: No, I always treated them with kindness and affection.

Q: Okay, do you take drugs?
A: No, I give them back.

Q: Come on, do you do drugs?
A: No, they do me.

Q: Which food makes you gag?
A: I don't eat food that makes me gag.

Q: What do you think of your favorite restaurant?
A: It's terrific! I give it Five Stars, Four Planets, Three Comets, Two Nova's, and a Molten Meteor.

Q: In one word, describe how you feel when watching the sunset?
A: Soular.

Q: As a little kid, what did you hate sharing?
A: Illicit substances, live ammo, smutty magazines, condoms, and the spoils of war.

Q: Name two things that have sparked joy in you in the past year?
A: One: Continuing to increase my net worth without working, and Two: Finding out specific people suffered misfortunes that they so richly deserved.

Q: Which is the best pizza topping?
A: A unique combination of blended raw aardvark bladder, charred wombat entrails, and dried tree bark marinated in cheap beer, scorpion juice, old mayonnaise, cayenne pepper, buttermilk, and cloves. No? How about marinara sauce then?

Q: Which subjects have you enjoyed the most this year?
A: As King of my own realm, I've enjoyed ruling all of my subjects and receiving their taxes along with their sworn fealty and homage.

Q: What is your favorite gemstone?
A: No favorite. I fancy them all equally and enjoy collecting a variety of them.

Q: What is one of your most unusual skills?
A: Long-distance subliminal seduction: I'm so good, you don't hear a thing!

Q: What is your favorite flower?
A: High-Grade Cannabis (pun intended).

Q: Who is your favorite actor?
A: Tom Hardy.

Q: Who is your favorite actress?
A: Michelle Yeoh

Q: Who is your favorite comedian?
A: Benny Hill.

Q: Who is your favorite modern philosopher?
A: George Carlin.

Q: Are you a morning person?
A: Yes, after 9 AM with sufficient quantities of caffeine and Sativa.

Q: What is the scariest creature in the world?
A: My ex-mother-in-law.

Q: Are you politically correct?
A: Hardly anything political is ever correct.

Q: Are you 'woke'?
A: No, I am Awake. There is a vast difference between the two.

Q: Are you a conspiracy theorist?
A: No, I'm not a conspiracy theorist nor even a conspiracy hypothesist; I'm just a conspiracy assumptionist: I assume that some conspiracies are false, some are true, and either way, I don't care, because they're distractions from what truly matters.

Q: Do you have any piercings?
A: Yes, my exceedingly intense, perturbingly piercing gaze and equally intense piercing sarcasm.

Q: Do you have any tattoos?
A: Yes, just one: the phrase '**TATTOOS ARE A WASTE OF MONEY**' in Uppercase Bold Size 72 Font running down the length of my cock.

Q: Are you trolling people?
A: No, I'm peopling trolls.

Q: Who is the greatest rock band of all time?
A: To put it into perspective, The Beatles created the arena in which all other bands play.

Q: Why don't you practice what you preach?
A: I don't practice what I preach because I'm not the type of person to whom I preach.

Q: What is your desired last meal on Earth?
A: A dozen ultra-potent marijuana edibles and four double-strength, double-sized Lemon Drop Martinis with ultra-expensive vodka, hand-squeezed real organic lemon and lime juice, raw cane sugar, shaken on ice, not stirred, and poured neat in a sugar-rim chilled glass, followed by a massive London Broil steak medium rare basted in Worcestershire sauce, garlic butter mash, creamed spinach, Yorkshire pudding, side salad, and crème brulee topped with a variety of berries, sweet sauce, and sprinkled with cinnamon and nutmeg for dessert. And a couple of large bong loads of a pure Indica for a happy ending.

Q: Don't Tell Anyone Else But...
A: You have a large, slimy tapeworm emerging from your anus.

Q: What is your most recent discovery?
A: Dehydrated H_2O—just add water, only $19.99!

Q: Are you a minimalist?
A: Yes, I am. I've 'minimalized' myself to one mansion, one yacht, one luxury vehicle, one wise self-managed investment portfolio including one metric tonne of gold, one large library, one huge 8K TV, one high-end audio system, one laptop, one outdoor hot tub, and sometimes sex with only one partner at a time.

Q: In one word, describe the last relationship you had with an American woman.
A: Hell.

Q: Which city is your ideal honeymoon?
A: Absolutely no marriage! I'm thrilled to be a rebel MGTOW on my terms in an awesome polyamorous relationship with an Asian mistress and several of her stunningly beautiful young open-minded, and incredibly naughty lady friends! I'm living the dream!

Q: Are you an atheist?
A: I'm more of an anti-theist, particularly on Saturdays.

Q: What is your religion?
A: Being rich.

Q: So many religions with so many deities. What is the true God of this world?
A: Money.

Q: Do you worship any divinities?
A: Yes, the Goddesses who are my mistresses.

Q: Are you a practicing warlock?
A: Yes, and I'm also a protective warlord.

Q: Are you a Freemason?
A: I'm an expensive May Sun.

Q: Are you a degenerate?
A: No, I'm a regenerate.

Q: What is the one snack that can always be found in your kitchen?
A: Ruru. She's delicious!

Q: Could you give me the inside interview about your personal life?
A: No, I won't do that; you can't afford me.

Share two truths and one lie:
1. I'm intelligent
2. The sun rises in the east
3. This statement is false

Q: If you could be any fictional character, who would it be?
A: Bible God.

Q: Are you for real?
A: I'm for real estate.

Q: Are you serious or joking?
A: When serious, I am sometimes joking, and when jesting, I can also be quite serious.

A Little More About Me

My Profile Headline:
Orgasm Donor. I give generously and frequently.

Preferred pronouns:
If you insist on playing that façade game suitable only for mentally-ill, daft peasants who deserve to be flogged in public, then you shall address me as Lord God; also, Your Majesty and Your Holiness will suffice, along with the obligatory genuflecting, effusive praises, terrific tributes, gushing accolades, and interminable bum-sucking. And do donate money to me. I like that.

When I'm Not Online:
For fun and profit, I occasionally levitate over various points in Oceania while bi-locating to various ports of call throughout the Universe and the astral plane.

Find Me In:
My private, secure ocean-side mansion, or yacht, or my gold-plated, gem-encrusted, glow-in-the-dark interstellar spaceship with plush, fully-stocked living quarters.

Q: Why I should buy your book?
A: Because obviously I'm channeling the voice of the Most High and reading notes from the Desk of God. And, I'm working strictly as an unpaid volunteer, but I get weekends and Mondays through Fridays off, free lunches, and paid male maternity leave thrice annually, which is good because I certainly need it!

Increase Your Intelligence

'Floccinaucinihilipilification' is the longest non-scientific word in the English language. It means the act of estimating someone or something as utterly worthless.

Use this word in a sentence to build your vocabulary. For example, "When I think of the majority of humans and their follies, I have a prevailing tendency towards floccinaucinihilipilification."

You see?

Review

Please leave a positive, glowing, gushing, enthusiastic, raving and even ranting Five Star review of this amazing, brilliant, superlative, magnificent book on your favorite book retailers.

And if you leave a bad review, I will viciously execrate you and all the mammals in your abode with perpetual maledictions including incurable inguinal diseases, random rectal bleeding, and perpetual constipation until you explode from your own ordure.

About The Author

Steve Sterling is a certified grand genius, modern philosopher, intrepid sybarite, profound philologist, epistemological warrior, sagacious iconoclast, brutally ruthless social commentator, cunning linguist, homily satirist, a marvelously malevolent misanthrope, and the reigning regent of hyperbole.

As an astonishingly brilliant anarchistic freethinker, he enjoys creating amazing aphorisms, crafting clever conundrums, hurling scathing denunciations and ridicule, and being a cheeky clever wit.

He is the first person in history to retrain Pavlov's dogs and free Schrödinger's cat from its theoretical limitations.

Sterling is able to subliminally communicate in three-and-a-half languages, leap lofty aspirations in a single bound, and thoroughly skewer everyone and everything he holds in disdain. He also has the striking distinction of being the third most acrimonious and truculent man in the world (but only on every second Tuesday before teatime).

He now divides his time between two residences: a remote atoll somewhere in the Pacific Ocean, and a small moon orbiting Jupiter.

This page does not exist.